Deer Have Fawns

by Elizabeth Dana Jaffe

Animals and Their Young

Content Adviser: Janann Jenner, Ph.D.

Science Adviser: Terrence E. Young Jr., M.Ed., M.L.S.,
Jefferson Parish (La.) Public Schools

Reading Adviser: Dr. Linda D. Labbo,
Department of Reading Education, College of Education,
The University of Georgia

COMPASS POINT BOOKS

Minneapolis, Minnesota

Compass Point Books
3722 West 50th Street, #115
Minneapolis, MN 55410

Visit Compass Point Books on the Internet at *www.compasspointbooks.com* or e-mail your request to *custserv@compasspointbooks.com*

Photographs ©: Gary W. Carter/Visuals Unlimited, cover; William J. Weber/Visuals Unlimited, 4; Cheryl A. Ertelt, 6; Mark J. Thomas/Photophile, 8; Rodney Todt/Visuals Unlimited, 10; Erwin & Peggy Bauer/Tom Stack & Associates, 12; Claudia Adams/Root Resources, 14; Robert McCaw, 16, 20; Alan G. Nelson/Root Resources, 18.

Editors: E. Russell Primm, Emily J. Dolbear, and Laura Driscoll
Photo Researchers: Svetlana Zhurkina and Jo Miller
Photo Selector: Linda S. Koutris
Designer: Bradfordesign, Inc.

Library of Congress Cataloging-in-Publication Data

Jaffe, Elizabeth Dana.
    Deer have fawns / by Elizabeth D. Jaffe.
       p. cm. — (Animals and their young)
    Includes bibliographical references (p.).
    Summary: Describes the birth, growth, development, and reproduction of deer.
    ISBN 0-7565-0169-5 (hardcover)
       1. Deer—Infancy—Juvenile literature. [1. Deer. 2. Animals—Infancy.] I. Title. II. Series.
QL737.U55 J35 2002
599.65—dc21   2001004132

Table of Contents

What Are Fawns?

Baby deer are called fawns. Deer are the only animals that have bones called **antlers** on their heads.

Deer live on every continent except Antarctica. Most deer live in forests.

There are about forty kinds of deer. Moose and reindeer are types of deer. This book is about white-tailed deer. They are common in North America.

A mother takes care of her newborn fawn.

What Happens Before Fawns Are Born?

An adult male deer is called a **buck**. An adult female deer is called a **doe**. Fawns grow inside the doe before they are born. She carries them for about 6½ to 7 months.

The mother deer gives birth to her fawns in the late spring. She looks for a safe, quiet place to have her babies.

◄ This buck is a white-tailed deer.

What Happens After Fawns Are Born?

Most mother deer give birth to two fawns at once. Each newborn fawn weighs about 5 to 8 pounds (2.3 to 3.6 kilograms).

The fawns are able to stand and walk after about forty-five to ninety minutes. Their legs are weak at first. They grow stronger after a few days.

◀ Fawns stand up and start walking soon after they are born.

How Do Fawns Feed?

Newborn deer **nurse** from their mother's body. They nurse every few hours.

Sometimes the doe goes off to find food for herself. While she is away, the fawns stay hidden. They lie still in the grass. The fawns come out to feed again when their mother returns.

A fawn drinks milk from its mother.

What Does a Fawn Look Like?

A fawn looks like a small version of its mother. It is covered with short, brown fur. It has a slim body and a short tail. Its four legs are long and thin.

Each foot has four toes. Over the two middle toes is a **hoof**. This hard covering protects the deer's toes.

Fawns look like their mother.

What Colors Are Fawns?

A newborn fawn has light, reddish brown fur with white spots. It blends in with its surroundings. This protects the fawn from other animals and humans. The fur on its chest and belly is white. So is the fur under its tail.

In the autumn, the fawn loses its spotted fur. It grows new grayish brown fur. Its new fur does not have spots.

A fawn has white spots on its back.

What Do Fawns Do and Eat?

When they are first born, fawns stay in a nest that is hidden in bushes. Four-week-old fawns begin to follow their mother everywhere. Does must always be careful. Wolves and bears hunt deer for food. The mother deer flicks her tail when she senses danger. This tells the fawns to hide.

When they are a few weeks old, fawns start to eat plants as well as milk. Deer do not eat meat. They like grass, leaves, berries, nuts, and twigs. Deer that live near farms may eat corn and other crops.

◀ This fawn is eating leaves.

What Happens As a Fawn Grows Older?

Many deer live in groups. The fawns in the group spend their days playing, sleeping, and eating. They also learn to use their sharp senses. Both adult deer and fawns can hear and smell very well.

As winter draws near, the fawns' fur gets thicker. They eat more food and grow stronger. This will help them live through the winter.

◀ This curious fawn checks out a squirrel!

When Is a Fawn Grown-up?

Most fawns stay with their mother for about a year. Then they can take care of themselves.

Some one-year-old does have fawns of their own. Most deer reach their full size by about five years old.

An adult deer is about 3½ feet (1 meter) tall from foot to shoulder. It weighs 100 to 300 pounds (45 to 136 kilograms). Bucks weigh more than does weigh. Deer live for about ten years in the wild.

◄ A full-grown buck

Glossary

antlers—the pair of bony growths on the top of a buck's head

buck—an adult male deer

doe—an adult female deer

hoof—the hard covering over a deer's middle toes

nurse—to drink milk produced by the mother

Did You Know?

- Scientists can tell how old a deer is by looking at its teeth. The teeth of older deer are more worn down.

- Some deer have such long tongues that they can use them to clean their eyes!

- Deer can run as fast as 40 miles (64 kilometers) per hour.

Want to Know More?

At the Library

Arnosky, Jim. *All About Deer*. New York: Scholastic Press, 1996.

Bare, Colleen Stanley. *Never Grab a Deer by the Ear*. New York: Cobblehill Books, 1993.

Wallace, Karen. *Wild Baby Animals*. New York: Dorling Kindersley, 2000.

On the Web

Environmental Education for Kids!: The White-tailed Deer

http://www.dnr.state.wi.us/org/caer/ce/eek/critter/mammal/fawn.htm

For fun facts about the white-tailed deer

Deer Domain: The Fawn Picture Page

http://www.deerdomain.com/fawn.htm

For photos of a newborn fawn

Through the Mail

National Wildlife Federation

Box FE76I001, 11100 Wildlife Center Drive

Reston, VA 20190-5362

To get information about a rare type of deer called the Key deer

On the Road

Elk Island National Park

Site 4, R.R. #1

Fort Saskatchewan, Alberta T8L 2N7

Canada

780/922-5790

To see deer, elk, moose, and other animals in the wild

Index

About the Author

After graduating from Brown University, Elizabeth Dana Jaffe received her master's degree in early education from Bank Street College of Education. Since then, she has written and edited educational materials. Elizabeth Dana Jaffe lives in New York City.